Praying Our Experiences

by

Joseph F. Schmidt, FSC

Saint Mary's Press
Christian Brothers Publications
Winona, Minnesota

PHOTOGRAPHY
Six cover photos, clockwise from top left: Jean-
Claude LeJeune, Jean-Claude LeJeune, Jack
Hamilton, Jack Hamilton, Jack Hamilton, Norman
Provost; frontispiece, Jack Hamilton; page 7, Phil
Kaczorowski; page 12, Norman Provost; page 17,
Paul Johnson; page 21, Ron Sievert; page 28,
Fortune Monte; page 35, Vernon Sigl; page 39,
Jack Hamilton; page 43, John Arms.

Fourth Printing—September 1982

ISBN: 0-88489-113-5

Contents

Introduction

Many of us sense that honest reflection on the ordinary experiences of our life has a prayer value. As we look over the times which have been occasions of spiritual growth for us, we realize that some of these times, perhaps even the majority, occurred when we took stock of ourselves and got in touch with the significance of an event in our life. It might have been the brief experience of a phone call from a friend at a time of grief, or the lengthy experience of years of discouragement and frustration. At the time, we may not have thought we were praying, but in retrospect we sense that all the elements of prayer were present: we felt the sinfulness of being ego-centered; we felt the graciousness of God's work in us; we felt, simply, the closeness of the Lord and the call to a deeper authenticity in our life. In this essay I wish to explore the implications of sincere reflection on our experience as a way of prayer, and I am calling this kind of reflection "praying our experiences."

To begin with I would like to make these observations:

1) By *experiences* I mean not only our sense awarenesses, but also much more. I want the word "experiences" to include not just happenings in their external aspects—the sight of a flower, the news of a war, the pain of an injury—but I want to include also who I am now as the person who has had this sensory awareness. By experiences, therefore, I mean to include also all the feelings, memories, and desires which are generated by the awareness.

5

2) By *praying* I mean offering in honesty and surrender the reality of myself and my life history to the Lord. This may sometimes take the form of a recited prayer formula, because some of these formulas may help to express my own feelings of longing to be in union with God. Often, however, praying our experiences will take the form of simple, direct, and very personal speaking to the Lord. Prayer formulas may not always appropriately and adequately convey the concrete content of the totally unique and private happenings of my life, nor can formulas always embody the very personal feelings of joy or anger I wish to express to the Lord.

3) By *praying our experiences*, then, I mean more than daydreaming, more than reminiscing, more than planning, more than pouting over the past. I mean getting in touch with who I am as the person who has had an experience and offering that "who" to God through reflection on that experience. I do not, however, wish to exclude daydreaming, reminiscing, planning, or pouting as experiences which themselves could be made the content of a prayer offering, nor do I mean that we pray only our good or joyful experiences. What I am advocating is that we pray *all* our experiences.

4) Praying our experiences is, I believe, a way of prayer which is valid and traditional. It is only one of many ways, and for some a preliminary way in the journey of prayerfulness, but it constantly recurs because it is so fundamental a way of praying. Although it could degenerate into self-centeredness (and fear of this might be the reason it is not often suggested or tried as a way of prayer), this form of prayer can lead, ultimately, to a depth of self-knowledge which purges self-centeredness.

5) Finally, I believe that praying one's experiences is exceedingly common among people who, ironically, not understanding it to be prayer, condemn themselves for not praying.

1
BEGINNING TO PRAY
OUR EXPERIENCES:
Notions of Prayer

Praying our experiences is the practice of reflecting on and entering honestly into our everyday experiences in order to become aware of God's Word in them, and to offer ourselves through them to God. We are getting in touch with who we are as people who have had personal experiences and are offering our whole selves to God through reflection on the events in our lives.

We pray our experiences when we use the content of our lived existence as the content of our prayer. Our memories and desires evoke the concrete happenings of our past as well as our plans and hopes for the future. These feelings and memories are the very focus of our prayer when we pray our experiences.

All of us have probably prayed this way, although we called it by another name. We called it "just thinking" when, on a sickbed, we spent restless and empty days pondering. We called it "questioning" when, after an experience of failure and despair, we passed sleepless nights asking "why?" We called it "resting" when we did nothing of consequence as we vacationed after a particularly stressful period. Yet, in retrospect, this time of thinking, questioning, and getting ourselves together may have been as helpful to our faith life as hours of formal prayer. We had indeed been praying our experiences, unfolding our memories and feelings in the presence of the Lord to see what our day-to-day living might be telling us and to what it might be calling us.

We may have been invited to such prayer, for example, by the chance word of a friend. We may have been taken aback by that word because it aroused in us feelings and memories out of proportion to its importance. We wonder at the power that the offhand remark had over us, and we are drawn not just to react to the intention or literal meaning of the speaker, but to enter into the significance of the sentiments and memories awakened in us.

A remark by an acquaintance may illumine part of ourselves which we had not seen so clearly before. Consider the following illustration. We are planning to make a retreat at a certain spiritual center which has been the site of so many graces before. We tell an acquaintance about our plans, and he or she comments offhandedly, "Oh, you want to be consoled by your friends again." The remark has power. We try to ignore it, but it does not go away. We reflect on this experience and recognize our need for the attention of others. The consolation and affection lavished by friends are more important to us than the quiet and solitude of the retreat setting. We may also sense a desire to be thought pious. Our wish to be closer to God is there, too, of course, but reflecting more on our deep response to the chance remark reveals with great clarity the ambiguity of our intention. We begin to unfold the implications of all this: what it says about our weaknesses and our strengths; what it says about past retreats; what it says about our relationships with those we call friends at the spiritual center; and what it says about our response to God's call. Thus, the remarks of others—whether complimentary, sarcastic, or merely offhanded —can be invitations to pray our experiences.

Further, our understanding of what prayer should be makes us uneasy when our own memories and feelings intrude during a time of prayer. Sometimes we take specific means to block out memories and feelings, believing that details of our life are not the proper content of prayer. We may have been taught that prayer is an activity quite sublime and otherworldly. We probably learned that in prayer we should talk to God about God. So we may consider prayer to involve some kind of mental image of God and to be focused on some kind of spiritual center outside of ourselves. Consequently, we ordinarily regard reflection on our experiences as an obstacle because it roots us to ourselves and prevents our flight to the desired level of communion with God. This, I believe, is a common but narrow way of viewing prayer.

We have been taught that only as a kind of last resort can our ordinary concerns and experiences be appropriate in prayer. Thus, if the memory of a friend arises during prayer we might say a brief prayer for the person, but we then return to our "proper" praying. If the memory of a moment of jealousy or pride comes to mind during prayer, if the remembrance of a childhood event or feelings of hurt and rejection fill us, we try to rid ourselves of these distractions and move back to our formal praying. We may even "baptize" our distractions by a brief moment of prayer if we cannot rid ourselves of them immediately.

Without being fully aware of all the implications, we may have simply defined memories and feelings out of our prayer. We may have named them distractions because we have decided that our prayer for today or for this week will be such and so, and these memories are, therefore, uncalled for. What I am suggesting, however, is to make these very "distractions" the content of our prayer—but not in order to solve problems, not to forward our projects, not to worry, not to do planning, not to

9

lick our wounds in self-pity. Rather, we focus on our experiences in order to get in touch with their revelatory power. We hear God's Word in them, and we are called to respond.

Praying our experiences is a form of prayer which may be particularly helpful at the end of a busy day. As we come to prayer at that time, our mind is filled with memories of projects and human encounters. We find ourselves flooded by the pleasant or humiliating feelings which arise from the memories of our behavior. If at this time we try to meditate on one of the mysteries in the life of Jesus, or open ourselves simply to the Lord's presence in imageless prayer, we will soon find ourselves in an impossible struggle. We will recall the harsh word we said so sarcastically during the day. We will recall our hurt pride at an admonition, or our anger at not being notified of a schedule change, or our joy at the phone call from a friend visiting town, or the kindness and patience we extended to a stranger.

If we look upon these as distractions to our prayer, then we will be constantly fighting them, and we may consider our prayer time to be a waste. But if we accept them as an integral part of our prayer, then our prayer can take on new aspects and power. We begin to know more clearly both the integrity and the brokenness of our motivation; we can sense more realistically our duplicity; we can become more aware of our goodness; we can see more sharply our values and priorities.

During this prayer we may not generate pious thoughts. We may not read Scripture. We may not use theological language in our reflection. We may not feel we are resting in the Lord. But in sensing the peace and the call which we know are the signs of yielding to God's presence in our life, we know we are praying.

Praying our experiences means being open to see ourselves as we are and to see our personal history—as it is known to the Lord. This requires an awareness and an honesty which will root us in our actual daily lives. It will lead us to talk to God about ourselves as we are in God's hands and will challenge us to growth through purifying self-knowledge. In other words, we recognize the Divine within ourselves rather than engage in some sublime and otherworldly activity of imagining a God out there.

Another impression we sometimes have about prayer is that since we pray for the sake of God's glory, we need not be overly concerned if our prayer does not produce any transformation in ourselves. We try to explain away the fact that our prayer is often ineffective in renewing our daily lives. Moreover, it seems contrived that various kinds of meditation require that we form a resolution to be carried out during the day for the sake of self-improvement. Praying our experiences, on the other hand, directly addresses the uneasiness we feel at the number of hours we have spent in formal prayer and the small effect these have had on our way of thinking and acting in daily life. In the process of praying our experiences, we resolve this dichotomy between our longing to glorify God and the process of our own transformation. When we pray our experiences we need not apply the meditation to ourselves; the meditation is about ourselves as we hold ourselves before the Lord in an offering of humility and resignation. Here, in our self-knowledge, we find the content of our praise, thanksgiving, and offering to God.

2
SELF-KNOWLEDGE:
Giftedness
and Brokenness

St. Teresa of Avila makes a significant comment about reflection on experiences and personal history. In her autobiography, Teresa tries to balance the need to go beyond self-knowledge in prayer with the continual need to return to it. She says, "This path of self-knowledge must never be abandoned, nor is there on this journey a soul so much a giant that it has no need to return often to the stage of an infant and a suckling. And this should never be forgotten. . . . There is no stage of prayer so sublime that it isn't necessary to return often to the beginning. Along this path of prayer, self-knowledge and the thought of one's sins is the bread with which all palates must be fed no matter how delicate they may be; they cannot be sustained without this bread."

Here Teresa insists that we must never close off the path of self-knowledge as a path of prayer. Considerations of heavenly things, the imaging of the Totally Other, or reflection on one of the mysteries of Jesus' life are all important ways into prayer, as is the elimination of all images in the total quiet of the Lord's presence. However, if we believe that these are the *only* paths of prayer, the thoughts of our own experiences will naturally appear to be distractions. Teresa's emphasis on "the bread" of self-knowledge can help us to a more expanded understanding of what prayer might be.

The Lord, as we know, wants the offering of ourselves. We sometimes fail to see, however, that this offering is not made in some abstract way with pious words or readings, but is rooted in the acceptance of the concrete details of our life. The offering of ourselves can only be the offering of our lived experience, because this alone is ourselves. In our prayer we take ourselves into our hands and offer to God our whole selves—our strengths and our weaknesses. As Teresa would say so simply, "this path of self-knowledge must never be abandoned."

Another reason why we must never abandon the path of self-knowledge is that authentic self-knowledge is not knowledge about our superficial ego. It is knowledge about our true self, and therefore it is knowledge about ourselves in relationship to humankind, to all of creation, and ultimately to God.

When we speak of authentic self-knowledge we are referring to the awareness of ourselves as we are in God's eyes. There is, therefore, no depth of self-knowledge without a depth of faith. Within this context of faith, self-knowledge grows and is understood as we become more aware of both our brokenness and our giftedness. Each of these aspects speaks not only of ourselves, but also of God as God relates to us.

Our giftedness speaks to us of God's goodness, because in our giftedness we come to know we have nothing which we have not received. In the context of faith the gifts of our talents, health, and friendships cry out to us of God. If a person believes that the love of a friend is merited, or that purity of motivation is the result of careful planning, he or she is probably someone with very superficial self-knowledge. These are gifts, pure and simple. It is far from the truth to believe that personal holiness can result from proper management of life details, or that trust in God is the fruit of personal strategy and effort. To the extent we have grown in faith and trust, to that extent we have been gifted. No amount of our own cleverness has produced it. As we grow in self-knowledge we begin to experience God's beneficence—until we at last realize that *all* of life is a gift.

We may also receive genuine appreciation from those with whom we live and work. They may say a word of thanks for the good we have done to them by our counsel, or they may tell us how much our friendship has meant to them. We acknowledge the good in ourselves, and yet often we are embarrassed. We feel that our efforts have not been great enough to warrant such gratitude. We know that our motivation has been tinged with selfishness. In praying these experiences, we become aware that the power going out from us to effect good in others originates well beyond ourselves. We begin to appreciate the power of the Spirit we now sense operating through us. Our patience, our gentleness, our understanding—all have been used by the God beyond us. The goodness of the Spirit has used our goodness, and we feel ourselves drawn to offer thanks to God for both.

The awareness of our sinfulness or brokenness also speaks to us of God for, paradoxically, our sinfulness is also a gift. Teresa says in referring to self-knowledge as a path of prayer: ". . . the thought of one's sins is the bread with which all palates must be fed." Our duplicity, our lust, our narcissism, our sloth— all speak to us of the fundamental brokenness in our lives. We know that no matter what our cleverness or strategies, in the face of this brokenness, we cannot rid ourselves of one speck of duplicity or one scintilla of narcissism. Sometimes we are frightened by the depth of our evil, and we try to ignore it. Yet, in paradox, our sinfulness becomes our bread. In a mysterious way we can be nourished by our own evil if we accept that evil as part of the truth about ourselves and offer that truth to the Lord.

St. Paul speaks of glorying in his weaknesses. He had reached a depth of self-knowledge that permitted him to understand that his righteousness consisted not in freedom from weakness and sin, but in being able to say *yes* to his entire life and his whole self. Paul knew that although a *yes* to life meant a *yes* to his own evil, it was also a *yes* to the God who in the evil was sustaining him in love and drawing him to good. For Paul the path of faith, not the way of works, was the right path to God, because he knew goodness is a gift of God, not something we can achieve by our own cleverness or effort.

Paul had the boldness to acknowledge that he had in the past and would continue in the future to do the things that he did not want to do. He knew he was a sinful person, one who would never reach that chimerical perfection of being fault-less. He sought rather that Christian holiness of being integral, of accepting into his offering to God his strengths and his weaknesses, his virtues and his sins. Paul offered his total self to God, not only what he would like to be, but what in truth he was. Offering ourselves in truth is the offering which God asks and which forms the basis of prayer.

In one of her letters, Thérèse of Lisieux revealed that she shared Paul's insight. "You are wrong," she wrote, "if you think your little Thérèse always marches with ardour along the way of virtue. She is weak, very weak; everyday she experiences it afresh. But . . . Jesus delights to teach her as he taught St. Paul, the science of glorying in one's infirmities. That is a great grace, and I beg Jesus to teach it to you, for in it alone is found peace and rest for the heart. Seeing yourself so worthless, you no longer wish to look at yourself, you look only at the sole Beloved."

Thérèse uses this awareness as the basis of her "little Way." "Perfection seems easy to me," she remarked. "I realize that it is sufficient that we acknowledge our nothingness and abandon ourselves like a child into the arms of our good Lord."

In our brokenness we come to know God's acceptance and love. In the depths of our hearts we sense God's Spirit acting toward healing and integration. Self-knowledge leads us to an awareness of both our evil and God's strength; an awareness which goes beyond what we could know from any theological formula. Thérèse acknowledged, "No book, no theologian taught this Way to me, and yet I feel in the depths of my heart that I possess the truth." We come to a knowledge similar to that which Paul, Mary Magdelene, and Peter had of Jesus and his way with sinners. In faith, self-knowledge leads us to a self-acceptance and a self-love which reach into an awareness of God's love.

Praying our experiences is a way into this depth of self-knowledge and acceptance. As we unfold our experiences and become aware of our blessedness and our brokenness, we begin to become more aware of the God who alone can fill all of our lives with graciousness.

3
INTROSPECTION:
Narcissism and
the Limited Ego

In the search of our experiences, in the unfolding of memories to learn of our weaknesses and giftedness, are we not in danger of focusing on ourselves in a narcissistic way? Are we not in the further danger of rationalizing and manipulating our experiences so they tell us what we want to hear?

These dangers are, of course, present; but they are dangers on the right road. We must move with some caution, but not turn back.

How can this unfolding of experiences avoid the dangers of narcissistic daydreaming on the one hand, and rationalizing or even denial of our memories on the other? When egoism and rationalization are already our primary approaches in life, these dangers are quite real—it becomes difficult to avoid narcissism in *anything* we do, even prayer. But if our life is being lived with reverence and purity of heart, then reflecting on our experiences will be steeped in this same reverence and purity. The life-stance with which we approach reflection, rather than the reflection itself, is crucial.

In this regard we may remember being warned against loving ourselves lest we fall into a form of selfishness. Now we have come to realize that loving ourselves is not at all selfish and that without loving ourselves we are seriously weakened in our human and spiritual growth. Loving ourselves is important in our full development and is the foundation of our love of others.

In the same way, seeing reflection on our personal history as a danger to raising our minds and hearts to God is a myopic view. Authentic reflection on life, like authentic love of self, is not the problem but part of the solution.

The very exercise of open and honest reflection will, in fact, help us to discern the extent to which selfishness and rationalization control our life-stance. It is a clue that we are indulging in unhealthy introspection when we find our ego is the source of energy and our small world is closing in on us. We then find ourselves judging the memory of our experiences in terms of our ego expectations and hopes; and events in our lives are labeled good or bad according to our own standards or those imposed on us. We find ourselves congratulating or reprimanding ourselves depending on whether we have appeared wise or foolish, powerful or weak, clever or obtuse, good or bad. Our reflections are not so much on what our experiences are saying to us, as on what we assess to be their value in enhancing our stature as successful persons or in crushing us as failures.

Narcissism makes our ego the center of our world and leads us away from honesty with ourselves. Narcissism prevents us from being receptive to the truth of our experiences. We close in on ourselves, not because reflection is dangerous, but because our stance is one of egocentrism. When we find ourselves not listening to our total experience but excluding part of it, or evaluating it according to our own expectations, then we can begin to suspect a narcissistic stance. When we dissect rather than receive; when we make our reflections ethical considerations of what should be, rather than faith awareness of what is; or when we manipulate our reflections by refusing to enter certain areas of our lives, even areas of religious piety and devotion, then to that extent we have placed conditions on our finding God's Word in our experiences.

We may also stifle the voice of our experience by controlling our memory and feeling with a refined rationalism. We rein in our imagination and muzzle our feelings. "Can anything good come out of Nazareth?" we ask, and we do not go to see. Our rational and analytic thought process becomes a barrier and leaves no crack for the unexpected inspiration or the surprise awareness. We have domesticated God, and our experiences cannot speak truth to us.

In this way we may be like the Pharisees who imposed their rationalism, their egos, and their Law on their experience of Jesus. Jesus' words of forgiveness and acts of healing were not seen as manifestations of God's power because Jesus' acts did not square with the Pharisees' analytic preconceptions. "If he were the Messiah he would know what kind of woman she is who is washing his feet." "The Messiah would not do such and so because we know what the Savior will and will not do." The natural feelings of sympathy and admiration that the Pharisees must have had for Jesus were stifled by their preconceptions. They left no room for the unexpected in their experience and so an awareness of God could not enter.

The Eastern mystical tradition is perhaps more conscious of this difficulty with preconceptions than is the Western popular spirituality. In some forms of Eastern discipline, in order to open the disciple's mind to the non-rational and to the unexpected, the religious master presents the spiritual novice with a *koan* as the focus for meditation. The *koan* is a statement or question which makes no sense. It usually includes elements which offer no coherent or reasonable basis from which an analysis can be made. The classic *koan* "What is the sound of one hand clapping?" contains elements which are themselves in contradiction, and so no reasonable answer by analysis is possible. And this is the point. In meditating on the *koan*, the novice, perhaps after months or years, comes to an awareness that rational analysis will not do, and that the answer, if there be an "answer," must come from beyond rationality and analysis, which is to say, from beyond the ego.

The understanding of the *koan* comes not from rationalizing or manipulating the data, but emerges in the ego's act of yielding to helplessness. It is not a matter of rationally "working" at the *koan*, therefore, that brings awareness. Rather being "in faith" with the *koan* leads to personal awareness and transformation.

In a similar way, we might say that many of our experiences are themselves *koans*. They contain elements which we see as contradictory and as making no sense: the death of a beloved child, failure in an area of special competence, a serious injury, falling in love. We ask ourselves for an answer or a meaning. We analyze and reason, but no understanding is forthcoming. And again, that is the point.

It is not by rational analysis or by the manipulation of the data of our experience that "the answer" will come, but by an egoless reflection in which we open ourselves to a source of power beyond ourselves. It is not by rationally "working" at the memory of our experiences that we gain awareness; rather, by being "in faith" with our experiences we grow to a sense of our finiteness and giftedness, and therefore to a sense of God's power and care. Reflecting on our experiences in a reverent way, far from being narcissistic, opens us to the source of life on the other side of our limited rational ego.

4
HEALING THE PAST:
Naming, Accepting, and Forgiving

All our experiences possess a revelatory power, yet we find ourselves unable to reflect on some of them. They are too disconcerting. They are too hurtful. We do not want to feel again the pain of the argument with a friend which ruptured a budding and precious relationship. We do not want ever again to feel the sense of rejection and loneliness which the memory of our relationship with our father or mother may bring. We resist reminders of our jealousy or our sensuality which have led us into spiteful and selfish acts. We do not want to think about our failure as a young teacher or our blunders in our first years of marriage. We do not want to reflect on how badly we handle human relationships and how slothful we are. We do not want to reopen wounds which have scarred over.

When we label these painful experiences "wounds," we must remember that this is *our* label. We say they are injuries to our sensitivities, to our expectations, to our hopes, to our sense of propriety and dignity and success; but as they manifest a part of the truth about ourselves, they are not wounds but facets of the precious totality of our lives. Our prayer will be hindered to the extent that we cannot gather up all of the reality of our lives into our offering to God.

Prayer is fundamentally an offering of ourselves to God. It is not a matter of offering the pious thoughts of theologians or spiritual writers. Nor is it a matter of offering to God only what we believe to be worthy of the Creator—our successes, our virtues, our goodness—as if they were our achievements to be given with a dignified obeisance. We offer to God who we are now: all of those longings for the Lord and all of those egotistical schemes that form part of our desires. All of this is part of us, and that is all we have to offer to God.

The parts of ourselves left out of our offering weaken our gift. God wants all of us, and so we work toward an integration of all of our memories and hopes into our total gift. To achieve this integrity requires that in some way the memories which cause pain and resistance must be healed.

When we refer to healing of memories, we are not speaking about morbidly dragging up hurtful experiences which have already settled. We are speaking of those painful experiences which are still with us and cry out for our attention. These memories come to us often by surprise. They recur when we least expect them. We do not drag them up, they come to our awareness of their own power, so to speak, because they have more to say to us. They are the memories which, like festering wounds, tell us they need attention.

In acknowledging our painful experience as part of our personal history, we begin to open ourselves to the possibility of being nourished by God through that experience. To the extent that we deny an experience, however hurtful, we deny God's loving care, which is mysteriously embedded in that experience.

Sometimes we may fear that if we even acknowledge a painful experience, it will gain control over us. We falsely imagine that if we simply "never think of it again" it will go away. This, of course, does not happen.

On the one hand, if an experience causes pain and disturbance when it comes to mind, we can be certain that it is disturbing us even when we are not aware of it. Casting an experience out of our memory does not cast its power out of our lives. By not acknowledging and accepting these painful memories we permit them to have power over us. We become bound by that part of our past. We are not free in relationship to it. We are defensive toward it, and we cannot be nourished by it.

On the other hand, this lack of freedom is also an indication of a blockage in our prayer. We have not yet gathered together all of ourselves in our offering to the Lord.

Rejecting the past as something "I'll never think of again" does not free us, but rather we free ourselves when we integrate our past into our total life history, so that our past and ourselves become one. The offering of ourselves to the Lord, then, approaches a completeness.

By ignoring painful experiences we are really allowing them to control us in a profound and subtle way. By acknowledging them we already begin to reduce their control and begin to gain power over them. A helpful example of this is the notion of "naming" in the Scriptures. God required Adam to name the animals before Adam could have dominion over them. This was a sign that Adam's relationship to the animals was one of freedom and power. When Jesus wished to manifest lordship over Peter, Jesus named Peter. For us, too, naming an experience gives us dominion over it, not by crushing it out, but by integrating it into our life as Adam accepted the animals into his world and as Jesus accepted Peter as a leader in the Church.

In acknowledging a painful experience, we begin the process

of healing because we begin the process of living the truth. This truth, Jesus assures us, will set us free, since it is enfolded in that most ultimate of truths: God's love. The process of healing of memories is primarily a process of letting the whole truth of our personal history be enfolded in the all-encompassing truth of God's love.

By our simple acknowledgment, we take the first step toward healing the pain of the memory. The second step is to broaden that acknowledgment into the feeling of acceptance, admitting both the experience and the pain as a part of ourselves.

At this point not only have we recognized that a painful experience does exist in our life, but we have begun to accept it as a significant one. We now begin to realize that, by its recurrence in memory and by the intensity of the related pain, the experience is asking to be brought to a reconciliation. This reconciliation begins when our relationship with the event shifts from that of an adversary (over-against) relationship to that of a dialogical (one-with) relationship. This shift indicates that we have come to a level of reverence and respect for the experience, realizing that it may speak truth to us. Prayer has often been described as listening to God; we may hear God if we open ourselves to hear what our painful experience has to say.

Our personal life will speak to us when we allow open quiet to follow our questions: what does this experience have to say about my way of living, my way of relating to others? What does this experience have to say about my priorities in life? What is the cause of the hurt? What would it require for the experience to no longer hurt? And what does all of this say about my ability to abandon myself "like a child into the arms of our good Lord"?

Further, moving from acknowledging a painful experience

to accepting it with reverence often calls for forgiveness. Frequently the pain itself is rooted in the need to forgive: we have not forgiven ourselves, and we have not forgiven others.

Perhaps the painful experience showed us our weakness or sinfulness. Perhaps our stupidity or sloth or self-centeredness motivated us to some foolish action we now sincerely regret. The memory brings with it a deep awareness of the sinfulness which is still with us. At times we cannot believe the Lord has already forgiven us, and we forget that Jesus asks us to forgive ourselves.

Perhaps the painful experience was caused by the cruelty of others, or by their insensitivity or their hatred toward us. Whether the problem lasted several minutes or several years, we are now called to forgive the other and to move our attention from the hurt to the Lord. We are asked to accept the reality that the Lord who loves both us and the other is offering us this memory as a way of getting closer to Jesus.

Forgiveness of ourselves and others does not require a rational justification; indeed it often will not bear one. But forgiveness does require faith in the power of the Lord's love to bring good out of evil. This faith will not be achieved merely by our rethinking the experience in our mind. Our reason fails because God's forgiveness and power are not encompassed by reason. Rather our faith is kindled in the quiet of imaging the Lord moving toward us, accepting us and others as Jesus accepted Zacchaeus and the adulterous woman. In our imagination we can experience what our reason fails to comprehend. Abandoning and going beyond reason, we can experience the warmth of the arms of our good Lord.

The forgiveness of ourselves and others allows us to accept more fully the memory of the experience as a part of ourselves.

We can now more completely incorporate the event as a part of our offering to the Lord. We now also begin to realize that the painful experience is a source of growth because it invites us to accept both our sinfulness and God's love.

The final step in the healing of memories that follows from acknowledgment and acceptance is appreciation. Memories are healed and our prayer is complete when we come full cycle and appreciate our painful experience. We reverently take up that hard rock of experience rejected by the builders within ourselves and accept it as the cornerstone of a new stage of growth.

We say yes, a grateful yes, to all that has been. We embrace our experience as a little death leading to a little resurrection. Redemptive suffering is most likely to be found not in the suffering of the body, nor in some romanticized oppression, but in the profound sadness of realizing our pettiness and self-pity and absolute poverty before God. Thérèse remarked: "To suffer our imperfections with patience, this is true sanctity." This is also the awareness of St. Paul when he prayed, "If I glory in anything it will be in my infirmities."

By healing of memories we mean accepting our experiences with all the associated pain, realizing that all things work together unto good for those who love God. By healing of memories we mean offering these experiences to God as our prayerful participation in that Paschal Mystery in which death is swallowed up in victory. By healing of memories we mean accepting into the treasury of self-giving to the Lord all of our experiences, especially those which have spoken to us so vividly of our vulnerability and sinfulness.

We know a memory has been healed when it speaks to us no longer of pain or brokenness but of God's mercy and love.

The memory has been healed when we can say what St. Thérèse says about the pain which her faults caused her: "The memory of my faults humbles me. It causes me never to rely on my own strength which is but weakness, but especially it teaches me the further lesson of the mercy and love of God."

When we pray our experiences we struggle to acknowledge, accept, forgive, integrate, and appreciate all of our personal history so that our prayer of offering might be complete. In the process we heal our memories because now those painful memories speak to us more of God's love than of our hurt.

5
WRITING:
Integration
and Discovery

But are we not trapped in the cycle of trying to purify our reflective stance by means of the same process of reflection? A step out of this dilemma is also a step toward addressing the previously mentioned danger of allowing reflection to be dominated by the ego, narcissistic daydreaming, or aimless reminiscing. This step is the process of writing out our reflections.

The writing of reflections helps us become more conscious of the full dimensions of our experience. It also helps us become more aware of the degree of our narcissism by allowing us to note more objectively where the center of our concerns lies. We cannot write of our experiences for any length of time or in any depth without noting what so clearly lies on the paper before us. Recurring judgments, values, and hopes, as well as descriptions of what we take to be our accomplishments and failures, speak to us of our primary life-stance. In our writing, our narcissism will surely manifest itself—as will our search for the deeper truth of our life.

At the same time, writing helps us to stop spinning the wheels of our anxiety and prevents us from jumping aboard the merry-go-round of our egotistical daydreaming. If we merely "think" of our experiences without writing some or all of them on paper, we sometimes find our reflection diffused, scattered, or diverted. We might also find ourselves rethinking the same question a hundred times.

If we are anxious or disturbed about the significance of an experience, the memory tends to return, mushrooming in confusion with each repetition. We begin to feel overwhelmed and disoriented. The experience quickly assumes unmanageable proportions, contaminating other memories. Writing, however, has the power to focus and locate experiences so they can be put into perspective within our total life and faith context. Juxtaposed in written form, experiences can be viewed in sequence, pattern, and proportion.

Writing our reflections also gives us an opportunity to move forward at our own pace in the exploration of very painful experiences by allowing us simply to list memories and feelings too difficult to be written or meditated on fully. We may sense that they have a deeper message for us, but they may still be too hurtful to unfold. Our feelings of jealousy or sexuality may be too embarrassing to explore, for example, or the memory of our acts of deceit and sloth too unsettling to consider fully. Even merely listed, the jottings of these experiences and feelings remain testimonies to our weakness and to our courage. We become aware of our fear and the power which the feelings and memories have over us, but at the same time we sense a message and know we will return sometime later to accept it more fully. Having simply named the experience, we know we can move on. In this way writing helps us in that process of healing of memories which we saw to be so essential for the offering of ourselves to God.

Further, writing helps us to open out those experiences and to search through those memories with which we are not immediately comfortable. We begin to see more clearly the patterns of choice leading into the experiences and the motivations and attitudes undergirding them. Gradually we become aware precisely of those elements of sinfulness and giftedness in our personal history in which we can especially recognize God's call.

Writing, however, may manifest its greatest power because of its creative and self-generating force. We do not merely put onto paper predetermined words and completed thoughts. Writing has the dynamic character of a movement into the unknown. It cannot fully be pre-controlled by our intellect, and therefore we can never be sure of what the writing might yield. When we take pen in hand we grasp a door handle and begin to open areas of our life history and present awareness which are deeper than we had imagined.

We write more than we are fully conscious of. We may write beyond what we had anticipated, and over the edge of our intellectual awareness. Under our pen emerge reflections and insights and awarenesses which we had not articulated before, but which we had always known to be true at a pre-reflective level.

When we have finished writing, or when we reread our writing months later, we may say a surprised but honest *yes* to what we have written. We apparently know much more than we can put into our conscious and orderly thought, and these preconscious understandings emerge as we write and later reread. In writing over the edge of our conscious insights, we often reach a level of awareness which we know to be a gift of God. What opens to us in self-knowledge we know to be beyond what we could have called forth by our own power.

In writing reflections on our experience we may also find that we are moved to engage in a kind of conversation. We find ourselves addressing the Lord directly in words of contrition and hope. "Lord, I want you; I need you. I'm sorry for my wrong doing; lead me." And we find ourselves writing a reply as from the lips of the Lord himself. "Why are you afraid? Trust me." Our conversation continues. "I fear giving in, Lord. I fear my deceit, my pride. I want to trust but cannot." "You know you can trust; I am with you." "But I am afraid, Lord; I am afraid to go too far. I want to control my life. I want to organize it." "Don't you think I can see the deepest desires of your heart?" "I want you, Lord, to be all in my life, but I hold back." "You don't have to do everything. I am with you." As our conversation continues we are startled by the truths which unfold. Significance and awareness reach a clarity which we had not realized consciously before. We see ourselves in a new light, perhaps in a way we had known in our hearts, but which we could not articulate before. Conversing with the Lord puts us in touch with depths in our experience we know to be true in the "world of the Lord" but which only now rise to conscious awareness. This insight often brings with it great consolation as we see our life in the hands of the Lord. On the other hand, it may also bring a sense of confrontation as we become aware of the force of our own duplicity. In recognizing here, often vividly, the blessedness of our life as well as the enormity of our own evil, we experience God's love and God's call.

Prior to our reflection, we may have judged an experience good or bad, a success or failure, extraordinary or common; but now labels are no longer significant. We are aware that by judging an experience we have classified its importance and therefore controlled its impact. In the process of labelling we have surrendered to the analysis of the ego and have manipulated our experience.

Bad and ordinary experiences, by their very classification, lose meaning and are relegated to marginal consideration. And yet Scripture speaks of a "felix culpa." Paul refers to glorying in "bad" experiences, and the gospel speaks of the signs of the Kingdom in the most ordinary happenings. Although some events in our life may have more immediate impact than others, and some may make us appear more successful than others, what is important is the realization that *every* experience has a religious dimension. At root, every experience embodies the challenge God offers us in love to become more integral and Christ-like.

Some may ask at this point whether the process of exploring our feelings and experiences in reflection and writing is prayer in the proper theological sense. Isn't prayer directed to God alone? Isn't it more properly thought of as a dialogue with the Totally Other?

We can approach an answer to these questions by taking seriously what we accept in faith to be certain. Nothing is more a gift from the Totally Other than our creation, our life, and our continued existence in Love. As a gift, our life unfolds under God's loving care. He continually sustains us, graces us, and calls us. Each of our days is a gift and a call from the Creator. To reflect on our experiences, then, is to unwrap the gift, to listen to the call. Far from being a narcissistic activity, this re-flection can be a way of being God-centered, a way of hearing God's Word addressed to us as individuals in the uniqueness of our person. It can be a way of taking seriously our faith in God's providence and our belief that all is grace.

The words of Thomas Merton are reassuring. In *Contemplative Prayer*, Merton writes that "our knowledge of God is para-doxically a knowledge not of him as object of our scrutiny, but of ourselves as utterly dependent on his saving and merciful knowledge of us. . . . We know him in and through ourselves in so far as his truth is the source of our being and his merciful love is the very heart of our life and existence." "By meditation," Merton remarks, "I penetrate the inmost ground of my life and seek the full understanding of God's will for me, of God's mercy to me, of my absolute dependence upon him."

Merton describes the aim of prayer much as we have described the aim of praying our experiences: "to come to know God through the realization that our very being is penetrated with his knowledge and love for us." "We know him." Merton adds, "in so far as we become aware of ourselves as known through and through by him." Here Merton describes prayer not so much as coming to know God or reaching to love God, but rather realizing that we are known and loved by God. That realization, I believe, rises vividly to consciousness as we enter into the process of praying our experiences.

Karl Rahner, in *Christian at the Crossroads*, puts the matter clearly when he suggests that speaking of prayer as a dialogue with the Totally Other is difficult to conceive if we understand by "dialogue" messages uttered by God as from an "outside source." Sudden impulses and insights in prayer, Rahner reminds us, can be explained as coming from our own psychic powers. For many persons, therefore, the notion of dialogue in prayer seems to be the same as "talking to ourselves." Rahner suggests that the concept of prayer as dialogue with the Totally Other can be more intelligible if we understand that "in prayer we experience ourselves as the ones spoken by God, as the ones arising from and decreed by God's sovereign freedom in the concreteness of our existence." In this way of understanding prayer "we are ourselves . . . the utterances and address of God which listens to itself." In *Contemplative Prayer*, Merton has expressed the same notion when he remarks, "I am myself a word spoken by God."

This means that in prayer we are neither on the one hand

dialoguing with an outside source who utters messages from without, nor are we simply talking to ourselves. We are reaching deeply into ourselves and sensing more clearly that we are in God's knowledge and love. We are discovering the Divine within us. We are experiencing ourselves and our lives as uttered by God, and we listen.

This listening is not a narcissistic activity because we are not simply listening to our own ego. Rather, we are opening ourselves to that dimension of our being and experience in which God speaks. We are not talking to ourselves in such a way that we are consciously controlling and manipulating our reflection.

When we speak of prayer as dialogue, then, we are referring to encountering those levels of ourselves and of our experiences which we do not control, because we have not formed them. They are not ours. We do not, in fact, even realize their existence until they manifest themselves. We do not possess these levels of experience; rather at these levels we are possessed—possessed by God's deep abiding love. The ego in narcissism cannot enter here, for the ego carries the baggage of ambition and fear, of defensiveness and schemes, which cannot be allowed at this level of self-knowledge.

In the book of Genesis God utters the Word and creation springs forth. Today we are that Word. Each of us is uttered in the uniqueness and actuality of our personal history. Our task is to hear that Word as it wells up in us from our being and experience. We listen to that Word with love and fear as we let it speak from our depths. Of what does this Word speak? It speaks of the giftedness of our life; it speaks of the brokenness of our life. It fills us with awe of God's blessings, and it calls us to deeper purity and love toward God and all creation. It reverberates with the Word of Scripture, which often helps us on our journey inward, but it now has the quality of our own unique and historical actuality.

6
SACRED SCRIPTURE:
Biblical Events
and Personal History

In our tradition all of Scripture is sacred to us, but only a very small fraction stirs and captures us. Some passages arouse in us such an emotional reaction that they cry out to be heard and we cannot be free of them. These passages have such power over us because they touch a part of us which reverberates with their message. These passages stir and capture us not because they are special in themselves, but because they have connected with a part of ourselves created by an experience now struggling to be unfolded. Scripture passages which may have meant little to us before suddenly become a powerful force because they light up and refocus our experiences.

The incident of Philip in the Gospel of John (John 1:43-46) illustrates how an experience can be illuminated by the Scriptures. Philip had, no doubt, read the Torah with reverence from his youth; yet only after his experience of encountering Jesus did the Scriptures come alive for Philip. Indeed, they become the light illuminating Philip's experience of Jesus. Until then the Scriptures had lacked that compelling force which now they possess for him. Philip sought out Nathanael, with whom he shared his enthusiasm: "We have found the one Moses spoke of in the law—the prophets too—Jesus, son of Joseph, from Nazareth" (John 1:45).

Another example of the Scriptures serving as a way into the depths of an experience is the account of the two disciples on the road to Emmaus (Luke 24:13-35). After that terrible and disheartening Friday, they were downcast. A stranger who had caught up to them as they walked consoles them by recalling to them passages from the Scriptures which referred to the Messiah. "Beginning, then, with Moses and all the prophets, he interpreted for them every passage of Scripture which referred to him" (Luke 24:27). No doubt the disciples had heard these Scriptures before without being captured by them. Even now, although they listened intently, they were not aware of the compelling power the Word was having on them. But after the stranger had vanished, then the Scriptures flamed out, and they realized their hearts had been burning within them as the stranger explained the Scriptures on the way. The Scriptures had illuminated and refocused that profound Friday experience, and they ran to tell the others.

As we read the Scriptures, some passages kindle our hearts. Our emotional response is our clue that this particular passage is addressed to us in a special way at this time in our life. We may have read the passage a hundred times before, but now it calls clearly and decisively. We are ready to be led into the depths of an experience, and the Scriptures will serve as our light.

Both for Philip and for the disciples on the road to Emmaus the Scriptures served as a light on their experience. They could then turn from the Scriptures to explore and treasure their experience. They, in a literal way, found in their experience what we in a symbolic way also encounter: the presence and the call of the Lord. As for Philip and the disciples, the Scriptures serve us by illuminating, clarifying, and evaluating our experiences. Often, like a true friend, the Scriptures reach into our hearts to arouse and to console by bringing out into the open memories and feelings which we may have scarcely known were there. These memories and feelings become the passage into the presence of the Lord in our life. The Scriptures call us, not to focus on the Scripture passages themselves, but to open ourselves to the Lord who lives and walks with us today.

Sometimes our respect for the Scriptures is so profound that we feel uneasy as we turn our attention from them to our experience. But in respecting them as a privileged expression of the Word of God, we should not fail to respect also our own experience as a privileged expression of that same Word of God. When we realize that the Scriptures themselves were written out of the experiences of the sacred authors and those of the community, we begin to view the events in our own lives with more reverence. The God who is revealed through the events recounted in the Scriptures is also revealed in our daily lives. This awareness makes less problematic our reflection on personal experiences as a way of knowing God's Word for us.

The sacred Scriptures were written within a given culture for a particular audience with a specific theological language and imagery. These situations have changed since the Scriptures were composed, and so we could not expect our experiences of God to duplicate those recorded in the Bible. Our experiences today have the mark of our personal and communal lives within a particular culture in the twentieth century. But we can expect that the sacred writings would shed light on these events and serve to help us explore and critique them.

The people of Israel sometimes confused their religious belief that God was faithful with their more rational hope that God would be consistent with their own understanding of history. We sometimes fall into the same trap. We can expect our experiences of God's call in our lives to be in accord with God's call to Israel, but we would do ourselves an injustice to assume that there will be no surprises in our life. One of the consistent elements of God's call to Israel was the invitation to accept the unexpected: "My ways are not your ways."

A closed attitude to how God might be present in our lives forces us to do violence to our experiences, just as such a closed attitude caused the Pharisees to reject and do violence to their experience of Jesus. Their misguided allegiance to a narrow understanding of Scripture and tradition resulted in their missing God present among them. The Pharisees assumed that any experience of the Messiah would fit their understanding of the Scriptures. They filtered personal experience through their reading of the holy Word. We can be victims of the same dangerous possibility if we fail to open ourselves to receiving the Lord in our daily lives.

Mary and the apostles read the same holy writings as the Pharisees, but they did not use them to prejudge their experiences. Mary and the apostles placed a supreme value on being available whenever and however God might call. In practice, they reverenced their experience and allowed it to become the path along which they walked with the Lord.

The Scriptures serve us best not when they become a filter through which we prejudge our experiences, but when they become our light and mirror. As our light, the Scriptures help us to clarify and explore our experiences. As our mirror, they help us to discover aspects in our experiences previously inaccessible to our gaze. Neither a light nor a mirror is used to best advantage if it is looked at for its own sake. Rather both are most helpful as means of illuminating and exploring. If we find ourselves using the Scriptures as an excuse for not exploring and treasuring our own experiences, then we can suspect that we do not understand the very best of the Good News: that God is lovingly present to us in our daily living.

By praying our experiences we come to know God's loving action in our daily lives. We can then begin to focus on these experiences as the content of our offering to the Lord. Frequently we will be led to understand more fully a particular experience by the light of the Scriptures, since the Scriptures can arouse us to the importance of an event and can move us into the depths of that experience. The Scriptures, however, will be misused in prayer if they cause us to do violence to our experience or to place no value on it. So, in praying our experiences, we need to use passages of Scripture to lead us back to our actual experiences, to illuminate them, and to enable us to explore and treasure them. In this way we may come closer to awareness of God's action in our life today.

7
MINISTRY:
Good Works, Love, and Ambiguity

St. John Baptist De La Salle, founder of the apostolic congregation of Brothers of the Christian Schools and himself a man considerably gifted in prayer, emphasized the value of doing good works as a means of spiritual growth. While encouraging his brothers to deeper levels of prayer, De La Salle was realistic enough to know that the brothers engaged in the ministry of education would often be preoccupied with their daily activities even during their time of prayer. He understood, moreover, that this preoccupation need not be a distraction, but could serve as the content of prayer.

De La Salle directed his teaching brothers to incorporate reflection about their ministry into their meditation. In his *Meditations for the Time of Retreat*, he remarks: "You must constantly represent the needs of your students to Jesus Christ, explaining to him the difficulties you experience in guarding them." De La Salle would certainly have his brothers pray for their students, asking God to give them the graces to avoid sin. But, further, he would have his brothers, as a form of prayer, directly reflect on their work in the schools. He recommended that the brothers speak to the Lord about those recurring difficulties they had in correcting their students.

Memories a brother might have of his angry reaction to a problem student, or his feelings of weakness and conflict as he tried to correct a student, or the pain of his attempts at reconciliation, or the indecisiveness of his efforts to divert a student from selfishness—these memories and feelings are to be laid out and explained to the Lord. The brother's prayer, therefore, might consist of unfolding these memories and allowing them to bring him to a deeper awareness of his motives, his values, his weaknesses, his power of love, and his force of hate.

De La Salle constantly returned to the need for the brothers to integrate their work and prayer, and praying experiences was one of the ways De La Salle understood the integration of ministry and prayer to take place. It was also one of the ways he believed the brothers would come to understand and purify their motives.

De La Salle warned, as have all the masters of the spiritual life, that we ought to be cautious of our best intentions. Those who reflect seriously on their good works often come to see the ambiguity of their motivations. "Examine before God," De La Salle recommends to those in ministry, "how you are acting in your ministry and whether you are failing in any of your responsibilities. Come to know yourself just as you are. Find fault with yourself accurately, unsparingly, so that when Jesus Christ comes to judge you, you will be able to face judgment without being afraid." We come to know ourselves just as we are when we reflect with honesty and openness on our experiences. To "examine before God how you are acting" is to enter the path of praying your experiences. It is a different way of saying what Teresa says about being sustained by the bread of the awareness of one's sins.

When we were adolescents we believed that loving people was rather a simple thing. Now that we are adults and have engaged in many good works and entered many relationships, we may be aware that we have seldom loved anyone. It is painful to realize our conflicting purposes and our selfishness, but it is also a nourishing awareness—for this honesty brings us closer to the true self we wish to accept and offer to the Lord.

When we were young we may have felt that we could easily do good works for God. It was, we may have imagined, only a matter of training and good intentions. Now that we are older we may be aware that most of our works have been done at least in part for ourselves. To gain status among our colleagues, to exert power over those with whom we were working, to express a talent for organization in our specialty—these may have been the motivations which have produced our successful project. People have praised us for our good works, and we cannot deny that our works have helped others to live more human and faithful lives. We cannot reject as evil our desire to develop our own talents, or to express our power of efficiency and organization. On the other hand, we know the ambiguity of our motivation, and as we come to know ourselves as we are, we are invited to "acknowledge our nothingness and abandon ourselves like a child into the arms of our good Lord." In such abandonment we "will be able to face his judgment without being afraid."

Involvement in doing good works is sometimes experienced as an obstacle to prayer. This will not be the case when our relationship to ministry and our experiences in ministry become the content of our prayer. As we pray our experiences of ministry, we resolve the dichotomy we may feel between involvement in works and prayer. Our ministry ceases to be a distraction to prayer and becomes the nourishment of prayer. Our work becomes the content of our prayer as our life becomes the focus of our offering to the Lord in faith.

8
FAITH:
Incarnation and Truth

Carl Jung wrote that he understood the greatest sin of faith to be that faith precluded experience. Jung was rightly rejecting a narrow view of faith. For some people faith does preclude experience, and we have seen that for others Scripture has that same effect. But we should be suspicious of anything—even an understanding of faith or Scripture or prayer—which suggests that we devalue the concrete, everyday realities in our lives. Incarnational faith, which is Christian faith, proclaims that in our unique and personal history God is active.

If faith meant solely and simply assent to certain doctrines, then faith would tend to distort and preclude experience. If faith meant that we held certain truths even in the face of developing knowledge and growing experience, then faith would be the negative force Jung rejected. But if we more rightly understand that by faith we do not hold truths so much as we are held by Truth, then faith calls us into our experiences, is a way of being present to them, a way of entering into their depths with trust and thanksgiving. Faith calls us not to preclude our experiences, but to include them in the Good News.

To what does faith call us through reflection on our experiences? Primarily we are called to realize in ourselves the Good

News: that God is lovingly present to us here and now. We are called to search out in our ordinary and confusing personal and communal history the truth which we glibly affirm in theory: that God's life flows into our life. In particular, we are called to become aware of our helplessness and brokenness on the one hand, and God's blessings and love on the other. We are called to realize that we are weak and sinful, limited and broken, yet blessed and graced and gifted. We are called to "acknowledge our nothingness and abandon ourselves like a child into the arms of our good Lord."

Our life history is the clay out of which this realization is fashioned. We are called to take our personal history seriously. The joys and struggles, the care and hurt both given and received, are all testimonies from our everyday life that God is in our lives and that we can trust ourselves in the presence of the Lord. We are invited to unfold these experiences and to let God's loving presence come through for our praise and gratitude. We are asked to offer ourselves to God as the person who has lived the history which is ours, and who has felt the personal experiences of brokenness and giftedness.

Sometimes a striking experience may startle us into an awareness of brokenness or blessedness. The death of a friend brings us to a realization of the preciousness of love and the beauty of friendship. We are also brought up short by an awareness of how shot through with narcissism our love has been. We recall the many acts of petty jealousy and the missed occasions when an affirmation or word of intimacy would have healed. We experience now in this death what Tillich calls a sure sign of our sinfulness: we recall the times when we rejoiced even in the suffering of our dearest friend. We experience, too, in the death of one we struggled to love, our own mortality and the pressing weight of our own death. These realizations strike with clarity and force. When they come upon us, we have come under God's Word judging us in our sinfulness and calling us to deeper integrity.

An experience of beauty and joy, or a moment of intimacy may also put us in touch with an awareness of God's love and blessing. We ride on a mountain road, or walk along a beach, or experience the affection and complete acceptance of a friend, and we suddenly awake to the realization that at work in our life is a force of love and care which fully encompasses us and all of reality. We see more clearly that we are loved quite undeservedly not just by a friend, but by Life. We become more aware that we and all of creation are being sustained and nourished by a beneficent free Love. And in this we realize God's Word uttered in blessing and care.

We could call experiences of such clarity and force "religious experiences" or "faith experiences" and then refer to other more ordinary experiences as "secular experiences." But this kind of distinction does not hold up. The experiences of God's presence under the aspects of judgment or love may come upon us most vividly in unique moments which are themselves gifts, but God's Word and presence are also available in the depths of all of our experiences. We would be closer to the truth to speak of the "religious or faith dimension" of every experience.

God is addressing us in all moments of life. We may experience some moments as more privileged than others because they reveal with more clarity and force our limitations and our giftedness. That this revelatory power is more apparent in some moments than others is due more to our own openness and readiness than to the intensity and availability of God's saving presence.

St. Teresa too refers to experience as revelatory of God's

Word. "Experience is a great help in all," she says in her autobiography, "for it teaches what is suitable for us; and God can be served in everything." And St. Thérèse says the same more succinctly, following St. Paul: "All is grace."

Our task, then, is to strip away those obstacles of egoism which block the truth of our experiences. Our faith calls us to search our experiences, to preclude none of them, to relish all of them, trying to reach that limit, that depth where the sound of God's Word of judgment and grace will become clear.

An Encouragement

Some will recognize what has been said about praying our experiences as a method which they have used off and on for many years. These persons may not be able to articulate why reflecting on their experiences felt like prayer, but they know it has filled their times of prayer and has been a source of the strength, confrontation, growth, and peace which have traditionally been associated with prayer. They also know that in this process they have been in the presence of the Lord of their life.

These persons may find encouragement in continuing to pray their experiences. They may also begin to notice sources other than the Scriptures or formal religious exercises impelling them into the depths of their experiences.

Earlier I mentioned the power of a random remark to call us to pray our experiences. The death of a friend, the awareness of beauty, or an impulse of anger may also compel us to pray in this way. This same power may be found in the passages of a novel, in the imagery of a poem, in moments of personal joy or grief, in the scenes of a movie, in the beauty of music, in times of playfulness, in the sounds of nature, in the details of a news article. Persons who are sensitive to the call of ordinary life situations are privileged indeed, because they are being invited to take seriously the truth that "God is not far from any one of us, for in him we live and act and have our existence."

Our life, we profess, is lived in God. There is no doubt that we can find God in the depth and flow of our own experiences. On occasion we will have to take formal times for this kind of reflection, but ultimately it is in the very process of living our daily existence that we are called to find God's Word and to offer ourselves in response. When we purify our stance toward life so that our narcissism is out of the way, and when at the center of our life are openness and reverence, then we will find one experience clarifying another, and all of our life revealing the caring presence of God and leading us to self-offering.

The greatest gift which we are asked to accept is the gift of living our life reverently. We are assured that Jesus came not that we may have more "prayers," or more reading of the Scriptures, or more pious devotions, or more of anything, but only "that (we) may live life and have it more abundantly."